Editor
Lorin Klistoff, M.A.

Managing Editor
Karen Goldfluss, M.S. Ed.

Editor-in-Chief
Sharon Coan, M.S. Ed.

Cover Artist
Barb Lorseyedi

Art Coordinator
Kevin Barnes

Art Director
CJae Froshay

Imaging
Rosa C. See

Product Manager
Phil Garcia

Publishers
Rachelle Cracchiolo, M.S. Ed.
Mary Dupuy Smith, M.S. Ed.

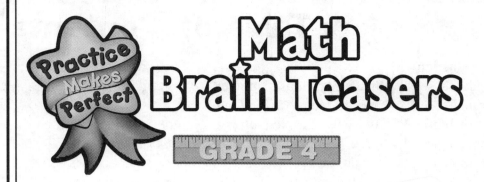

Math Brain Teasers

GRADE 4

Author

Mary Rosenberg

Teacher Created Materials, Inc.
6421 Industry Way
Westminster, CA 92683
www.teachercreated.com
ISBN-0-7439-3754-6

©*2003 Teacher Created Materials, Inc.*
Reprinted, 2003
Made in U.S.A.

Table of Contents

Introduction. 3
Brain Teaser 1: What's My House Number? (*using logic*) 4
Brain Teaser 2: Favorite Meals (*using logic*) 5
Brain Teaser 3: Crossword Puzzle (*solving equations*). 6
Brain Teaser 4: Name That Number! (*solving number trivia*) 7
Brain Teaser 5: Alphabet Codes (*solving equations*) 8
Brain Teaser 6: Find the Primes! (*identifying prime numbers*). 9
Brain Teaser 7: What Comes Next? (*identifying number patterns*) 10
Brain Teaser 8: What's the Rule? (*identifying number patterns*) 11
Brain Teaser 9: Stamp Collecting (*working with money*) 12
Brain Teaser 10: Wheels-R-Us (*adding money*) 13
Brain Teaser 11: Money Riddles (*working with money*) 14
Brain Teaser 12: More Money Riddles (*working with money*) 15
Brain Teaser 13: The Change Machine (*working with money*) 16
Brain Teaser 14: Change It Again! (*working with money*) 17
Brain Teaser 15: Deals! Deals! (*working with money*) 19
Brain Teaser 16: Circles of Challenge Set A (*adding two and three digits*). 20
Brain Teaser 17: Circles of Challenge Set B (*subtracting one and two digits*) 21
Brain Teaser 18: Circles of Challenge Set C (*subtracting one, two, and three digits*). 22
Brain Teaser 19: Circles of Challenge Set D (*multiplying one and two digits*) 23
Brain Teaser 20: Circles of Challenge Set E (*multiplying one and two digits*) 24
Brain Teaser 21: Circles of Challenge Set F (*dividing by one and two digits*). 25
Brain Teaser 22: What's Missing? (*solving equations*). 26
Brain Teaser 23: More Missing Numbers (*solving equations*) 27
Brain Teaser 24: Math Matters (*using operations*) 28
Brain Teaser 25: More Math Matters (*using operations*) 29
Brain Teaser 26: Mystery A (*using logic*) 30
Brain Teaser 27: Mystery B (*using logic*) 31
Brain Teaser 28: Mystery C (*using logic*) 32
Brain Teaser 29: Mystery D (*using logic*) 33
Brain Teaser 30: Mystery E (*using logic*) 34
Brain Teaser 31: Roman Numeral Fun (*writing Roman numerals*) 35
Brain Teaser 32: The Roman Way (*recognizing and writing Roman numerals*) 36
Brain Teaser 33: Roman Rule (*recognizing number patterns*) 37
Brain Teaser 34: Name That Movie! (*adding four digits*) 38
Brain Teaser 35: Name That Cartoon! (*adding four digits*) 39
Brain Teaser 36: Community Garden (*finding the perimeter and area*). 40
Brain Teaser 37: The Right Amount of Space (*finding the area*) 41
Brain Teaser 38: Paint by Numbers (*finding the sums of areas*). 42
Brain Teaser 39: Dandy Division Squares (*working with division*) 43
Brain Teaser 40: More Dandy Division Squares (*working with division*) 44
Brain Teaser 41: Magical Multiplication (*working with multiplication*) 45
Brain Teaser 42: More Magical Multiplication (*working with multiplication*). 46
Answer Key 47

Introduction

The old adage "practice makes perfect" can really hold true for your child and his or her education. The more practice and exposure your child has with concepts being taught in school, the more success he or she is likely to find. For many parents, knowing how to help your children can be frustrating because the resources may not be readily available. As a parent it is also difficult to know where to focus your efforts so that the extra practice your child receives at home supports what he or she is learning in school.

This book has been designed to help parents and teachers reinforce basic skills with children. *Practice Makes Perfect* reviews basic math skills for children in grade 4. This book contains 42 brain teasers that allow children to learn, review, and reinforce math concepts. Brain teasers have long proved their worth as vehicles of learning. Such activities carry with them curiosity and delight. While it would be impossible to include all concepts taught in grade 4 in this book, the following basic objectives are reinforced through the brain teasers:

- uses logic
- solves equations
- identifies prime numbers
- identifies number patterns
- works with money
- adds two, three, and four digits

- subtracts one, two, and three digits
- multiplies by one and two digits
- divides by one and two digits
- uses operations
- recognizes and writes Roman numerals
- finds the perimeter and area

How to Make the Most of This Book

Here are some useful ideas for optimizing the activity pages in this book:

- Set aside a specific place in your home to work on the activity pages. Keep it neat and tidy with materials on hand.

- Set up a certain time of day to work on the brain teasers. This will establish consistency. Look for times in your day or week that are less hectic and more conducive to practicing skills.

- Keep all practice sessions with your child positive and constructive.

- Help with instructions, if necessary. If your child is having difficulty understanding what to do or how to get started, work through the first problem with him or her.

- Review the work your child has done. This serves as reinforcement and provides further practice.

- Allow your child to use whatever writing instruments he or she prefers. For example, colored pencils can add variety and pleasure to the activity page.

- Pay attention to the areas that your child has the most difficulty. Provide extra guidance and exercises in those areas.

- Look for ways to make real-life applications to the skills being reinforced.

Brain Teaser 1

What's My House Number?

Read each clue. Use the chart below. If the answer to the clue is "yes," make an "O" in the box. If the answer is "no," make an "X" in the box. Then answer the statements below the chart.

Clues

- Marie's house number has only odd numbers in it.
- Jay's house number has more even numbers than odd numbers.
- Shep's house number is evenly divisible by 3.
- Larry's house number is evenly divisible by 10.

		61	276	810	954	977
Jay		O	X	X	X	X
Tina		X	X	X	O	X
Larry		X	X	O	X	X
Shep		X	O	X	X	X
Marie		X	X	X	X	O

1. Jay's house number is ___61___.

2. Tina's house number is ___954___.

3. Marie's house number is ___977___.

4. Larry's house number is ___810___.

5. Shep's house number is ___276___.

Brain Teaser 2 ⟋ ❧ ❧ ❧ ❧ ❧ ❧ ❧ ❧ ❧ ❧ ❧

Favorite Meals

Read each clue. Use the chart below. If the answer is "yes," make an "O" in the box. If the answer is "no," make an "X" in the box. Then answer the statements below the chart.

Clues

- Tina likes to drink water when she has tacos for lunch.
- Jay never eats hot dogs but he does like shakes.
- Marie always has a soda when she eats pizza.

	Hamburger	Pizza	Hot dog	Taco	Shake	Soda	Water	Milk
Shep			O					O
Jay	O				O			
Tina				O			O	
Marie		O				O		

1. Shep eats __Hot Dogs__ and drinks __milk.__ .

2. Jay eats __Hamburgers__ and drinks __shakes__ .

3. Tina eats __tacos__ and drinks __water__ .

4. Marie eats __pizza__ and drinks __soda__ .

Brain Teaser 3

Crossword Puzzle

Solve each problem. Write the number word on the crossword puzzle.

ten	eleven	twelve	thirteen	fourteen	fifteen
sixteen	seventeen	eighteen	nineteen	twenty	

Across

1. 12 + 5   **9.** 6 x 3

6. 73 − 62   **10.** 100 ÷ 5

8. 6 + 7

Down

1. 64 ÷ 4   **4.** 7 x 2

2. 96 ÷ 8   **5.** 5 x 2

3. 85 − 70   **7.** 51 − 32

Brain Teaser 4 ꙮ ꙮ ꙮ ꙮ ꙮ ꙮ ꙮ ꙮ ꙮ ꙮ ꙮ ꙮ

Name That Number!

Write the number.

1. Days in a week: _____

2. Months in a year: _____

3. In a dozen: _____

4. In a baker's dozen: _____

5. In a trio: _____

6. In a pair: _____

7. Seconds in an hour: _____

8. Hours in a day: _____

9. Hands on a clock: _____

10. In a gross: _____

11. In a zip code: _____

12. Fingers on one hand: _____

13. Toes on both feet: _____

14. Stripes in the U.S. flag: _____

15. Stars on the U.S. flag: _____

16. Years in a decade: _____

17. Days in one year: _____

18. Days in a leap year: _____

19. Days in a school week: _____

20. Days in a weekend: _____

Use the numbers above to write and solve each problem.

21. Months in one year ÷ In a dozen: _____

22. Seconds in an hour ÷ In a trio: _____

23. Days in a leap year – Days in a year: _____

24. Years in a decade x Days in a weekend: _____

25. Stripes in a flag x Days in a week: _____

26. Number of toes on both feet ÷ Number of fingers on one hand: _____

27. In a gross + Hands on a clock: _____

28. Hours in a day – Days in a school week: _____

Brain Teaser 5

Alphabet Codes

Add the letters in each day of the week to find the value of the word.

A = 22	F = 26	K = 20	P = 21	U = 23	Z = 3
B = 4	G = 10	L = 6	Q = 7	V = 8	
C = 9	H = 25	M = 16	R = 2	W = 18	
D = 14	I = 15	N = 11	S = 12	X = 13	
E = 19	J = 5	O = 1	T= 17	Y = 24	

1. Sunday:_____

2. Monday: _____

3. Tuesday: _____

4. Wednesday: _____

5. Thursday: _____

6. Friday: _____

7. Saturday: _____

Use the value of each word to solve the math problems.

8. Sunday x 4 – Thursday =_____

9. (Saturday – Tuesday) x 20 = _____

10. (Wednesday – Friday) ÷ 10 = _____

11. Monday ÷ 4 x Sunday = _____

12. (Saturday – Friday) + (Wednesday – Monday) = _____

#3754 *Practice Makes Perfect: Math Brain Teasers*

Brain Teaser 6

Find the Primes!

Color the prime numbers blue. Color the remaining numbers purple.

28	16	70	9	24	42	10	21	81	30
55	48	71	11	54	75	31	53	38	14
15	72	29	47	18	25	73	7	82	20
36	60	21	69	84	62	92	25	75	24
88	9	68	40	90	34	49	22	93	4
14	87	26	8	5	13	94	8	18	63
16	55	20	45	58	12	66	12	50	9
86	22	80	65	35	27	16	85	26	44
46	3	99	18	12	4	95	56	1	15
78	43	23	98	24	96	15	59	17	51
27	57	19	61	79	67	41	37	64	21
8	39	77	10	26	76	16	52	12	32

Brain Teaser 7

What Comes Next?

Finish each pattern and write the rule.

1. 3, 8, 13, 18, 23, _____ , _____ , _____ , _____ , _____ , _____

The rule is: _____

2. 27, 25, 23, 21, 19, _____ , _____ , _____ , _____ , _____ , _____

The rule is: _____

3. 71, 67, 63, 59, 55, _____ , _____ , _____ , _____ , _____ , _____

The rule is: _____

4. 35, 43, 51, 59, 67, _____ , _____ , _____ , _____ , _____ , _____

The rule is: _____

5. 25, 37, 49, 61, 73, _____ , _____ , _____ , _____ , _____ , _____

The rule is: _____

6. 49, 59, 69, 79, 89, _____ , _____ , _____ , _____ , _____ , _____

The rule is: _____

7. 8, 15, 22, 29, 36, _____ , _____ , _____ , _____ , _____ , _____

The rule is: _____

Brain Teaser 8 ꙮ ꙮ ꙮ ꙮ ꙮ ꙮ ꙮ ꙮ ꙮ ꙮ ꙮ

What's the Rule?

Look at each pattern. Write the rule.

1. 75   150   300   600   1,200   2,400   4,800   9,600

The rule is: _____

2. 10   50   250   1,250   6,250   31,250

The rule is: _____

3. 7,290   2,430   810   270   90   30   10

The rule is: _____

4. 12,800   6,400   3,200   1,600   800   400   200   100

The rule is: _____

5. 35   140   560   2,240   8,960   35,840   143,360

The rule is: _____

6. 13   130   1,300   13,000   130,000   1,300,000

The rule is: _____

Brain Teaser 9 ᗧ ᗧ ᗧ ᗧ ᗧ ᗧ ᗧ ᗧ ᗧ ᗧ ᗧ ᗧ ᗧ

Stamp Collecting

Use the chart to answer the questions.

Stamp Sets		Tools and Accessories	
Movie stars	$9.11	Magnifying glass	$0.71
Authors	$1.51	Tweezers	$2.43
Singers	$6.25	Glue	$1.01
Presidents	$8.10	Album	$6.74
Cartoon characters	$9.98	Extra album pages	$0.73 ea.
Teddy bears	$8.93	Plastic stamp sleeves	$0.33 ea.

1. Manuela has $1.42. How many plastic sleeves can she buy?

_____

2. How much money will she have left? _____

3. Ira has $9.65. Does he have enough money to buy a set of tweezers and an Authors stamp set? _____

4. Bentia has $2.22. She was given $1.49 in change. What item did she buy?

_____

5. Rolf wants to buy an album and a bottle of stamp glue. How much money does he need?

Rolf needs _____.

6. Sabrina bought 2 different stamp sets for a total of $18.91. Which stamp sets did she buy?

_____

7. Jason spent $6.74 on an album. Jeremy spent $3.24 more than Jason. What item did Jeremy buy?

_____

#3754 Practice Makes Perfect: Math Brain Teasers © *Teacher Created Materials, Inc.*

Brain Teaser 10 ଚ ଚ ଚ ଚ ଚ ଚ ଚ ଚ ଚ ଚ ଚ ଚ

Wheels-R-Us

Use the chart to answer the questions.

Unicycle
$2.53

Bicycle
$4.12

Tricycle
$6.38

Skateboard
$1.03

Scooter
$4.51

Roller Blades
$7.17

Roller Skates
$5.15

Wagon
$6.27

---

1. Jennifer bought a unicycle and a pair of roller blades. She was given $9.65 in change. How much money did Jennifer have?

Jennifer had _____ .

2. Roger bought a scooter and a bicycle. He was given $9.89 in change. How much money did Roger have?

Roger had _____ .

3. Simon bought a tricycle and a scooter. He was given $4.84 in change. How much money did Simon have?

Simon had _____ .

4. Irene bought a skateboard and a wagon. She was given $8.46 in change. How much money did Irene have?

Irene had _____ .

5. Susan bought a wagon, a unicycle, and a scooter. She was given $0.38 in change. How much money did she have?

Susan had _____ .

6. Amit bought a pair of roller blades, a tricycle, and a skateboard. He was given $0.36 in change. How much money did he have?

Amit had _____ .

Brain Teaser 11 ⟋ ⟋ ⟋ ⟋ ⟋ ⟋ ⟋ ⟋ ⟋ ⟋ ⟋

Money Riddles

Solve each riddle. Circle the answer.

1. Joanie has 3 dimes and 3 nickels. Ryan has 3 quarters. Who has more money? Joanie Ryan	**2.** Sam has 2 quarters, 2 nickels, and 2 dimes. Sarah has 2 half-dollars. Who has more money? Sam Sarah
3. Geraldo has 6 dimes. Sybil has half that number of half-dollar coins. Who has more money? Geraldo Sybil	**4.** Marlow has 4 dimes, 1 quarter, and 3 pennies. Janice has 2 quarters, 2 dimes, and 2 pennies. Who has more money? Marlow Janice
5. Robin has 4 half-dollars. Michael has 4 quarters and 4 nickels. Who has more money? Robin Michael	**6.** Christopher found $1.00. Cassie found 1 half-dollar, 1 quarter, 1 dime, 1 nickel, and 1 penny. Who found the most money? Christopher Cassie
7. Cheryl put $2.36 into her piggy bank. Anthony put a dollar bill, 6 nickels, and 2 dimes into his piggy bank. Who put more money into a piggy bank? Cheryl Anthony	**8.** Bonnie had $3.69 in her pocket. Mark had 5 half-dollars and 5 nickels in his pocket. Who had more money? Bonnie Mark

Brain Teaser 12

More Money Riddles

Solve each riddle.

A. Preston has 5 coins. Paige has half as much money as Preston. Paige has $0.27.

1. How much money does Preston have?

Preston has _____ .

2. What coins does Preston have?

Preston has the following coins:

_____ pennies _____ nickels

_____ dimes _____ quarters

_____ half-dollars

B. Nan has 8 coins. Brady has $1.98. Brady has three times the amount of money that Nan has.

1. How much money does Nan have?

Nan has _____ .

2. What coins does Nan have?

Nan has the following coins:

_____ pennies _____ nickels

_____ dimes _____ quarters

_____ half-dollars

C. Vern has 8 coins. Allison has twice the amount of money that Vern has. Allison has $2.36.

1. How much money does Vern have?

Vern has _____ .

2. What coins does Vern have?

Vern has the following coins:

_____ pennies _____ nickels

_____ dimes _____ quarters

_____ half-dollars

D. Rochelle has 10 coins. Ricky has 1/3 the amount of money that Rochelle has. Ricky has $0.81.

1. How much money does Rochelle have?

Rochelle has _____ .

2. What coins does Rochelle have?

Rochelle has the following coins:

_____ pennies _____ nickels

_____ dimes _____ quarters

_____ half-dollars

Brain Teaser 13 ⟳ ⟳ ⟳ ⟳ ⟳ ⟳ ⟳ ⟳ ⟳ ⟳ ⟳ ⟳ ⟳

The Change Machine

Solve each riddle.

The Change Machine	
You Put In	**You Receive**
1 Dime ⟶	$0.05
1 Quarter ⟶	$0.20
1 Half-dollar ⟶	$0.40
$1.00 bill ⟶	$0.85
$5.00 bill ⟶	$4.75
$10.00 bill ⟶	$9.80
$20.00 bill ⟶	$19.50

A. Marcie puts 4 quarters in the machine.

1. How much money is she given in return? _____

2. How much money did she have to pay to use the machine? _____

B. Bill puts a dollar bill in the machine.

1. How much money is he given in return? _____

2. How much money did he have to pay to use the machine? _____

C. Vivian puts 3 half-dollars in the machine.

1. How much money is she given in return? _____

2. How much money did she have to pay to use the machine? _____

D. Stu puts a $5 dollar bill in the machine.

1. How much money is he given in return? _____

2. How much money did he have to play to use the machine? _____

E. Catarina puts two $1.00 bills in the machine.

1. How much money is she given in return? _____

2. How much money did she have to pay to use the machine? _____

F. Ernie puts 10 dimes in the machine.

1. How much money is he given in return? _____

2. How much money did he have to pay to use the machine? _____

Brain Teaser 14 ⟳ ⟳ ⟳ ⟳ ⟳ ⟳ ⟳ ⟳ ⟳ ⟳ ⟳

Change It Again!

Figure out how many times each amount of money can be put back into the machine. How much money will be left? The first one is done for you.

The Change Machine

You Put In	You Receive
1 Dime ⟶	$0.05
1 Quarter ⟶	$0.20
1 Half-dollar ⟶	$0.40
$1.00 bill ⟶	$0.85
$5.00 bill ⟶	$4.75
$10.00 bill ⟶	$9.80
$20.00 bill ⟶	$19.50

Example: one $1.00 bill

This is the change received from $1.00.

This is the change received for each coin.

$1.00

Q   Q   Q   D

This is the change received for each coin.

D D D D D D

N N N N N N N

___7___ nickels or $ ___0.35___

---

1. $0.10

_____ nickel or $ _____

---

2. $0.25

_____ nickels or $ _____

---

3. $0.50 (half-dollar coin)

_____ nickels or $ _____

Brain Teaser 14

Change It Again! *(cont.)*

Use the information on page 17 to help you complete these problems.

4. $1.50 ($1 bill and 2 quarters) _____ nickels or $ _____	**5.** $1.50 ($1 bill and a half-dollar coin) _____ nickels or $ _____
6. $0.75 (3 quarters) _____ nickels or $ _____	**7.** $1.00 (2 half-dollar coins) _____ nickels or $ _____
8. $0.50 (5 dimes) _____ nickels or $ _____	**9.** $1.00 (4 quarters) _____ nickels or $ _____

Brain Teaser 15

Deals! Deals!

Find the better deal. Circle the answer. Then find the difference between the two amounts.

The Change Machine

You Put In		You Receive
1 Dime	→	$0.05
1 Quarter	→	$0.20
1 Half-dollar	→	$0.40
$1.00 bill	→	$0.85
$5.00 bill	→	$4.75
$10.00 bill	→	$9.80
$20.00 bill	→	$19.50

Example: $1.00 or 4 quarters

$0.85 or 4 x $0.20 = $0.80

(\$1.00)   4 quarters

The difference is $0.05

---

1. 6 quarters or 15 dimes

_____ or _____

6 quarters   15 dimes

The difference is $ _____.

---

2. 8 quarters or two $1.00 bills

_____ or _____

8 quarters   two $1.00 bills

The difference is $ _____.

---

3. $5.00 bill or five $1.00 bills

_____ or _____

$5.00 bill   five $1.00 bills

The difference is $ _____.

---

4. $10.00 bill or ten $1.00 bills

_____ or _____

$10.00 bill   ten $1.00 bills

The difference is $ _____.

---

5. $20.00 bill or two $10.00 bills

_____ or _____

$20.00 bill   two $10.00 bills

The difference is $ _____.

Brain Teaser 16

Circles of Challenge Set A

Each circle has a specific value. The sum is where two (or more) circles overlap. Find the value of each circle. The first circle has been started for you.

Circles of Challenge #1

Values: 25, 50, 75, 100, 125

The number 100 added to 50 equals 150.

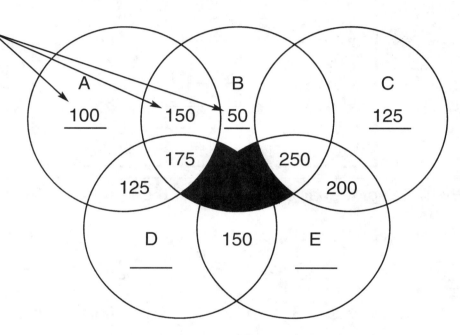

Circles of Challenge #2

Values: 100, 200, 300, 400, 500

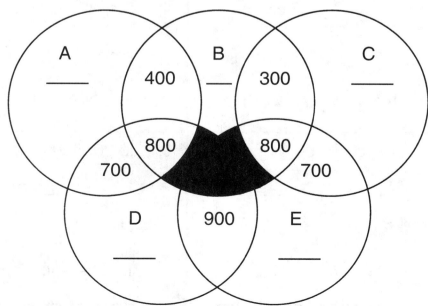

Brain Teaser 17

Circles of Challenge Set B

Each circle has a specific value. The difference is where two (or more) circles overlap. Find the value of each circle. The first one has been started for you.

Circles of Challenge #3

The number 19 subtracted from 20 equals 1.

Values: 20, 19, 18, 17, 16

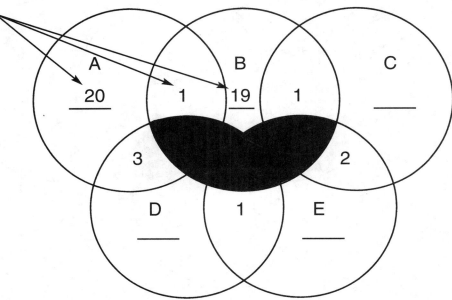

Circles of Challenge #4

Values: 50, 40, 30, 20, 10

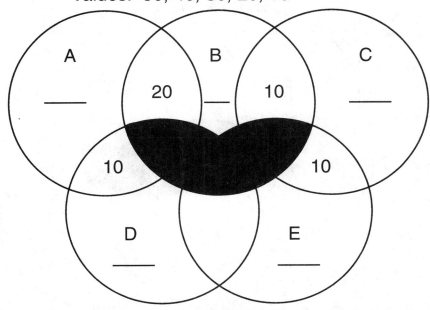

Brain Teaser 18

Circles of Challenge Set C

Each circle has a specific value. The difference is where two (or more) circles overlap. Find the value of each circle. The first one has been started for you.

Circles of Challenge #5

The number 15 subtracted from 20 equals 5.

Values: 20, 15, 10, 5, 0

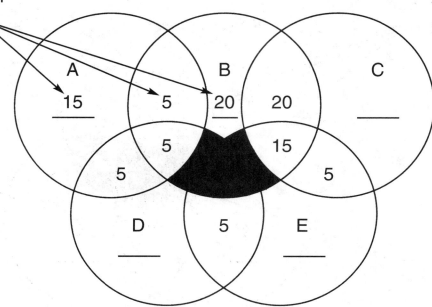

Circles of Challenge #6

Values: 250, 200, 150, 100, 50

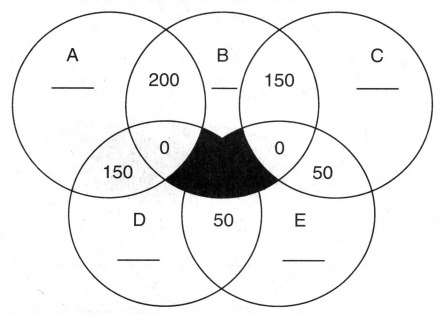

Brain Teaser 19 ⤳ ❥ ⤳ ❥ ⤳ ❥ ⤳ ❥ ⤳ ❥ ⤳ ❥

Circles of Challenge Set D

Each circle has a specific value. The product is where two (or more) circles overlap. Find the value of each circle. The first one has been started for you.

Circles of Challenge #7

The number 4 multiplied by 3 equals 12.

Values: 1, 2, 3, 4, 5

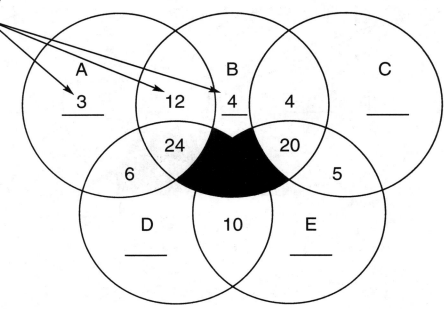

Circles of Challenge #8

Values: 2, 4, 6, 8, 10

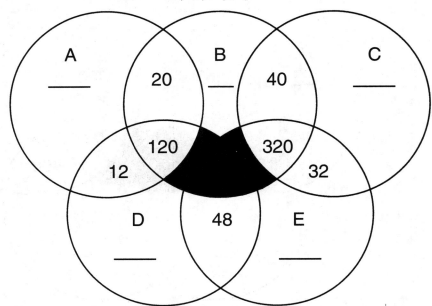

Brain Teaser 20

Circles of Challenge Set E

Each circle has a specific value. The product is where two (or more) circles overlap. Find the value of each circle. The first one is started for you.

Circles of Challenge #9

The number 5 multiplied by 15 equals 75.

Values: 5, 10, 15, 20, 25

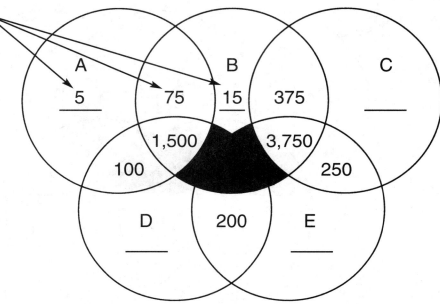

Circles of Challenge #10

Values: 10, 20, 30, 40, 50

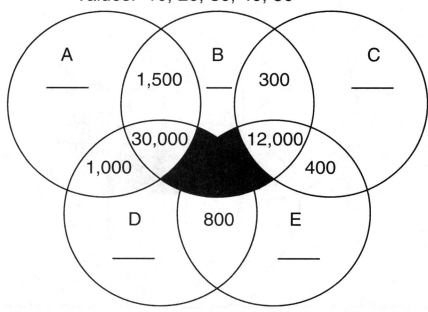

Brain Teaser 21

Circles of Challenge Set F

Each circle has a specific value. The quotient is where two (or more) circles overlap. Find the value of each circle. The first one is started for you.

Circles of Challenge #11

The number 32 divided by 8 equals 4.

Values: 2, 4, 8, 16, 32

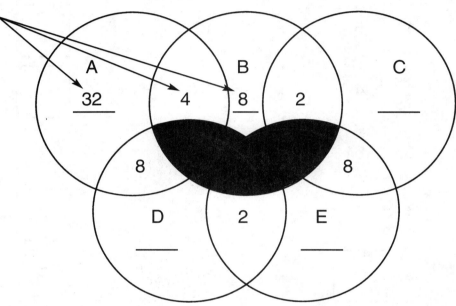

Circles of Challenge #12

Values: 3, 6, 12, 24, 36

Brain Teaser 22 ◑ ◑ ◑ ◑ ◑ ◑ ◑ ◑ ◑ ◑ ◑

What's Missing?

Write the missing number for each problem. Each number can be used only one time.

51	52	53	54	55	56	57	58	59	60

1.   5   x   12   =   ☐

2.   4   x   13   =   ☐

3.   61   −   ☐   =   2

4.   28   +   28   =   ☐

5.   ☐   ÷   11   =   5

6.   9   x   6   =   ☐

7.   ☐   ÷   3   =   17

8.   39   +   ☐   =   92

9.   ☐   −   23   =   34

10.   29   x   2   =   ☐

Brain Teaser 23 ⊙ ⊙ ⊙ ⊙ ⊙ ⊙ ⊙ ⊙ ⊙ ⊙ ⊙

More Missing Numbers

Write the missing number for each problem. Each number can be used only one time.

| 91 | 92 | 93 | 94 | 95 | 96 | 97 | 98 | 99 | 100 |

1. 100 x 1 – 0 = ☐

2. 3 x 31 = ☐

3. 8 x 12 = ☐

4. 742 + ☐ = 837

5. ☐ ÷ 7 = 14

6. 10 x ☐ = 990

7. 351 – ☐ = 260

8. ☐ ÷ 2 = 46

9. 510 – ☐ = 413

10. 9 x 10 + 4 = ☐

Brain Teaser 24

Math Matters

Write the missing sign (+, −, ÷, x).

1.	5 ☐ 5 = 25	**2.**	8 ☐ 4 = 2
	5 ☐ 5 = 0		8 ☐ 4 = 4
	5 ☐ 5 = 10		8 ☐ 4 = 32
	5 ☐ 5 = 1		8 ☐ 4 = 12
3.	16 ☐ 4 = 64	**4.**	66 ☐ 6 = 60
	16 ☐ 4 = 4		66 ☐ 6 = 396
	16 ☐ 4 = 12		66 ☐ 6 = 72
	16 ☐ 4 = 20		66 ☐ 6 = 11
5.	32 ☐ 8 = 24	**6.**	48 ☐ 3 = 144
	32 ☐ 8 = 4		48 ☐ 3 = 51
	32 ☐ 8 = 40		48 ☐ 3 = 16
	32 ☐ 8 = 256		48 ☐ 3 = 45
7.	52 ☐ 2 = 50	**8.**	54 ☐ 9 = 63
	52 ☐ 2 = 26		54 ☐ 9 = 45
	52 ☐ 2 = 104		54 ☐ 9 = 6
	52 ☐ 2 = 54		54 ☐ 9 = 486

Brain Teaser 25 ∂ ☙ ∂ ☙ ∂ ☙ ∂ ☙ ∂ ∂ ☙

More Math Matters

Write the missing sign (+, −, ÷, x).

1.	730 ☐ 10 = 740		**2.**	108 ☐ 3 = 105
	730 ☐ 10 = 7,300			108 ☐ 3 = 36
	730 ☐ 10 = 73			108 ☐ 3 = 111
	730 ☐ 10 = 720			108 ☐ 3 = 324
3.	534 ☐ 2 = 267		**4.**	459 ☐ 9 = 450
	534 ☐ 2 = 532			459 ☐ 9 = 51
	534 ☐ 2 = 536			459 ☐ 9 = 4,131
	534 ☐ 2 = 1,068			459 ☐ 9 = 468
5.	620 ☐ 4 = 2,480		**6.**	995 ☐ 5 = 199
	620 ☐ 4 = 616			995 ☐ 5 = 1,000
	620 ☐ 4 = 155			995 ☐ 5 = 4,975
	620 ☐ 4 = 624			995 ☐ 5 = 990
7.	336 ☐ 6 = 342		**8.**	329 ☐ 7 = 322
	336 ☐ 6 = 330			329 ☐ 7 = 47
	336 ☐ 6 = 56			329 ☐ 7 = 2,303
	336 ☐ 6 = 2,016			329 ☐ 7 = 336

Brain Teaser 26 ✺ ✺ ✺ ✺ ✺ ✺ ✺ ✺ ✺ ✺ ✺

Mystery A

Follow the clues to discover the mystery number.

75	31	35	10	36
41	84	86	53	22
49	99	88	18	17
27	93	46	94	11
24	29	57	52	31

Cross off all numbers that are the following:

- divisible by 9
- multiples of 5
- have two even digits
- have two odd digits
- have two digits when multiplied together equal 36
- when one digit is subtracted from the other the difference is 3

What is the mystery number? _____

Brain Teaser 27 ⟳ ⟳ ⟳ ⟳ ⟳ ⟳ ⟳ ⟳ ⟳ ⟳ ⟳

Mystery B

Follow the clues to discover the mystery number.

21	18	81	37	46
10	19	41	34	12
45	56	31	51	82
95	97	75	55	46
76	72	83	98	69

Cross off all numbers that are the following:

- have the same digits

- divisible by 3

- less than 50

- greater than 60

What is the mystery number? _____

Brain Teaser 28 ᕫ ᕬ ᕫ ᕬ ᕫ ᕬ ᕫ ᕬ ᕫ ᕬ

Mystery C

Follow the clues to discover the mystery number.

558	346	891	626	324
191	310	223	594	628
777	818	125	813	899
412	541	946	310	715
461	837	675	576	241

Cross off all numbers that are the following:

- contain all odd or all even digits
- have a 3 as one of the digits
- have a number larger than 5 in the tens place
- have a number smaller than 5 in the hundreds place
- divisible by 9
- even numbers

What is the mystery number? _____

Brain Teaser 29 ⟡ ⟡ ⟡ ⟡ ⟡ ⟡ ⟡ ⟡ ⟡ ⟡ ⟡

Mystery D

Follow the clues to discover the mystery number.

2,569	4,693	2,777	1,052	7,763
8,691	8,105	6,789	1,138	3,453
5,351	4,910	1,479	4,679	1,031
8,894	5,214	2,131	1,282	8,456
1,059	3,761	2,325	8,103	1,010

Cross off all numbers that are the following:

- larger than 5,000
- have more even than odd digits
- have more odd than even digits
- divisible by 5
- have 2 consecutive odd or even digits
- divisible by 7

What is the mystery number? _____

Brain Teaser 30 ೨ ✇ ✇ ೨ ✇ ೨ ✇ ೨ ✇ ೨ ೨ ✇

Mystery E

Follow the clues to discover the mystery number.

77,176	69,746	63,849	42,122	10,582
10,289	35,795	44,661	15,678	14,938
48,473	53,981	21,869	62,816	61,497
79,746	12,573	31,077	10,785	85,531
31,424	62,122	15,281	53,586	78,495

Cross off all numbers that are the following:

- have all odd digits
- when all the digits in the number are added together, they have a sum greater than 25
- when all the digits in the number are multiplied, they have a product greater than 50
- even numbers
- divisible by 5
- divisible by 9

What is the mystery number? _____

Brain Teaser 31 ౩ ☙ ౩ ☙ ౩ ☙ ౩ ☙ ౩ ☙ ౩ ౩ ☙

Roman Numeral Fun

The Romans used 7 letters to represent all numbers—except for 0. Write each number using Roman numerals.

I	V	X	L	C	D	M
1	5	10	50	100	500	1,000

6: _____

2: _____

1: _____

12: _____

15: _____

86: _____

21: _____

60: _____

73: _____

815: _____

281: _____

356: _____

686: _____

783: _____

127: _____

770: _____

530: _____

762: _____

2,163: _____

3,573: _____

3,107: _____

1,078: _____

2,510: _____

3,898: _____

4,103: _____

1,200: _____

Brain Teaser 32 ∂ ☺ ∂ ☺ ∂ ☺ ∂ ☺ ∂ ☺ ∂ ∂ ☺

The Roman Way

To show one, ten, or a hundred less, write the smaller number first. It means to subtract that amount from the larger number.

I	V	X	L	C	D	M
1	5	10	50	100	500	1,000

Write each number using Arabic (regular) numerals.

1. IV: _____

2. XIV: _____

3. XXIV: _____

4. XLVIII: _____

5. XCV: _____

6. XL:_____

7. XC: _____

8. LXIV: _____

9. LXIX: _____

10. DIX: _____

11. CLIV: _____

12. CIX: _____

13. CIV: _____

14. CM:_____

15. CD:_____

16. MXXIX:_____

17. DCCCIV:_____

18. DLIV: _____

Write each number using Roman numerals.

A. 24: _____

B. 90: _____

C. 39: _____

D. 41: _____

Brain Teaser 33 ꙮ ꙮ ꙮ ꙮ ꙮ ꙮ ꙮ ꙮ ꙮ ꙮ

Roman Rule

Write the rule for each pattern.

1. I, III, V, VII, IX, XI, XIII, XV, XVII, XIX

The rule is: _____

2. I, VI, XI, XVI, XXI, XXVI, XXXI, XXXVI

The rule is: _____

3. XXX, XXXIII, XXXVI, XXXIX, XLII, XLV, XLVIII, LI

The rule is: _____

4. X, XX, XXX, XL, L, LX, LXX, LXXX, XC, C

The rule is: _____

5. L, LVIII, LXIV, LXXII, LXXX, LXXXVIII, XCVI, CIV

The rule is: _____

6. L, C, CL, CC, CCL, CCC, CCCL, CD, CDL, D, DL, DC, DCL, DCC

The rule is: _____

7. I, II, IV, VIII, XVI, XXXII, LXIV, CXXVIII, CCLVI

The rule is: _____

Brain Teaser 34 ꙮ ꙮ ꙮ ꙮ ꙮ ꙮ ꙮ ꙮ ꙮ ꙮ ꙮ ꙮ

Name That Movie!

In 1903, one of the first successful feature-length movies was produced. What was the name of that movie? To discover the answer, find the sum for each one of the math problems. Write the letter that matches each sum on the line.

1. 2,101 + 2,416	2. 4,943 + 8,123	3. 4,278 + 7,696	4. 9,101 + 9,456	5. 3,198 + 1,553	6. 4,772 + 8,323
A	B	E	G	H	I

7. 6,579 + 1,568	8. 2,937 + 3,797	9. 2,584 + 5,108	10. 1,081 + 1,654	11. 2,101 + 9,769
N	O	R	T	Y

____ ____ ____   ____ ____ ____ ____ ____
2,735 4,751 11,974   18,557 7,692 11,974 4,517 2,735

____ ____ ____ ____ ____
2,735 7,692 4,517 13,095 8,147

____ ____ ____ ____ ____ ____ ____
7,692 6,734 13,066 13,066 11,974 7,692 11,870

Brain Teaser 35 ⟳ ⟳ ⟳ ⟳ ⟳ ⟳ ⟳ ⟳ ⟳ ⟳ ⟳

Name That Cartoon!

In 1928, Walt Disney released his first animated cartoon. What was the name of that cartoon? To discover the answer, find the sum for each one of the math problems. Write the letter that matches each sum on the line.

1. 2,546 + 6,766	**2.** 3,172 + 9,512	**3.** 3,892 + 1,010	**4.** 1,346 + 1,610	**5.** 9,881 + 7,545
A	B	E	I	L
6. 2,110 + 8,794	**7.** 9,734 + 7,132	**8.** 5,510 + 4,682	**9.** 8,393 + 4,931	**10.** 5,851 + 6,278
M	O	S	T	W

___ ___ ___ ___ ___ ___ ___ ___ ___

10,192 13,324 4,902 9,312 10,904 12,684 16,866 9,312 13,324

___ ___ ___ ___ ___ ___

12,129 2,956 17,426 17,426 2,956 4,902

#3754 Practice Makes Perfect: Math Brain Teasers

Brain Teaser 36

Community Garden

Peas

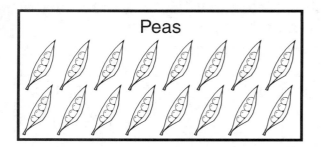

Cucumbers

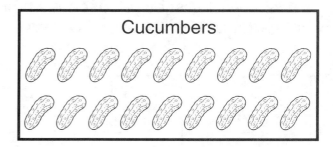

Carrots

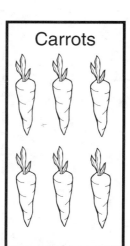

Beans

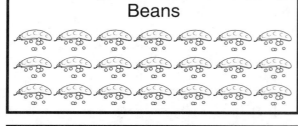

Lettuce

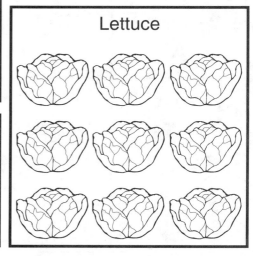

Potatoes

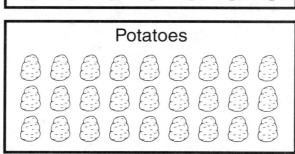

Find the perimeter and area for each kind of vegetable. Each vegetable equals 1 unit.

Vegetable	Perimeter	Area
Example: Carrots	3 + 2 + 3 + 2 = 10 units	3 x 2 = 6 sq. units
1. Beans		
2. Potatoes		
3. Lettuce		
4. Peas		
5. Cucumbers		

Brain Teaser 37

The Right Amount of Space

Find the correct amount of area for each animal. Write the letter on the line.

Legend

☐ = 1 foot

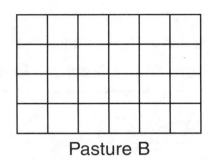

Pasture B

Pasture C

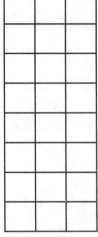

Pasture E

Pasture A

Pasture D

1. Gertie Giraffe needs at least 20 square feet. Which pastures would be a good fit for Gertie? Pastures _____ and _____	**2.** Harry Hamster likes a nice, cozy space. Any pasture with less than 5 square feet would be a good fit for Harry. Which pasture would Harry like the best? Pasture _____
3. Roberta Rattlesnake likes to slither in a space that has more than 6 square feet but less than 24 square feet. Which pasture would be a good fit for Roberta? Pasture _____	**4.** Larry Ladybug likes a pasture that has one square foot for each one of his legs. Which pasture would be a good fit for Larry Ladybug? Pasture _____

Brain Teaser 38

Paint By Numbers

Decide how much paint each person needs to buy. Circle the correct amount.

| 1/2 gallon = 100 square feet |
| 1 gallon = 200 square feet |
| 5 gallons = 1,000 square feet |

1. Janice wants to paint the dresser. (The dresser is 3' wide, 2' deep, and 5' high.)

   1/2 gallon

   1 gallon

   5 gallons

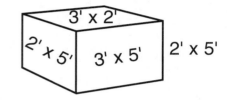

2. Ned wants to paint his bedroom. (Ned's bedroom has a ceiling that is 10' x 10'. Each of the 4 walls is 10' x 9')

   1/2 gallon

   1 gallon

   5 gallons

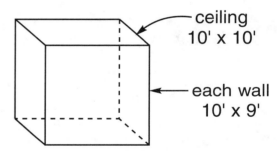

3. Reba wants to paint a wall in the garage. (The wall is 25' long and 8' high.)

   1/2 gallon

   1 gallon

   5 gallons

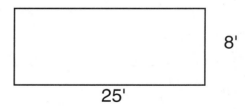

4. Ralph wants to paint the pool. (The pool is 6' deep, 20' long, and 10' wide.)

   1/2 gallon

   1 gallon

   5 gallons

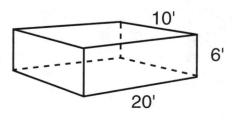

Brain Teaser 39 ⟳ ⟳ ⟳ ⟳ ⟳ ⟳ ⟳ ⟳ ⟳ ⟳ ⟳ ⟳

Dandy Division Squares

Divide going across and down. Write the missing numbers. Study the example.

Example

÷ →		
12	3	4
6	3	2
2	1	2

Square #1

÷ →		
30		5
	2	
3		1

Square #2

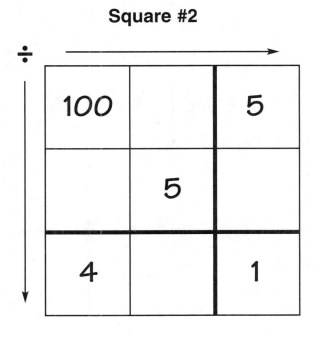

÷ →		
100		5
	5	
4		1

Square #3

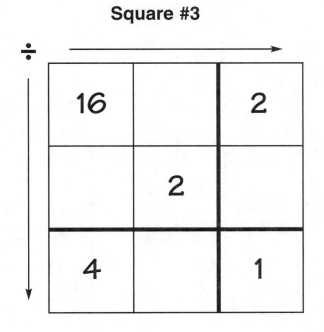

÷ →		
16		2
	2	
4		1

Brain Teaser 40

More Dandy Division Squares

Divide going across and down. Write the missing numbers. Study the example.

Example

÷	→	
48	8	6
12	4	3
4	2	2

Square #1

÷	→	
64		4
	4	
8		2

Square #2

÷	→	
120		3
	20	
2		1

Square #3

÷	→	
200		4
	10	
5		1

Brain Teaser 41

Magical Multiplication

Multiply going across and down. Write the missing numbers. Study the example.

Example

X →
↓

5	5	25
6	2	12
30	10	300

Square #1

X →
↓

2		14
	5	
12		420

Square #2

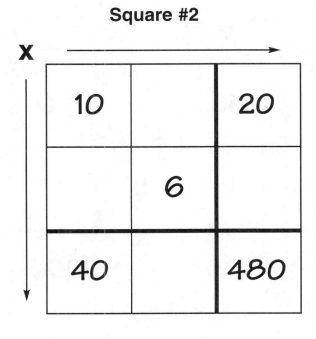

Square #3

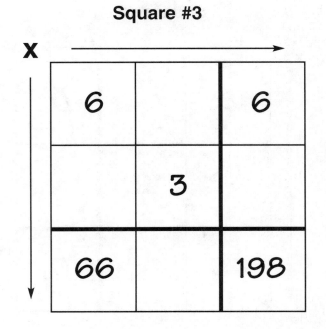

Brain Teaser 42

More Magical Multiplication

Multiply going across and down. Write the missing numbers. Study the example.

Example

X →		
3	4	12
6	5	30
18	20	360

Square #1

X →		
9		27
	1	
36		108

Square #2

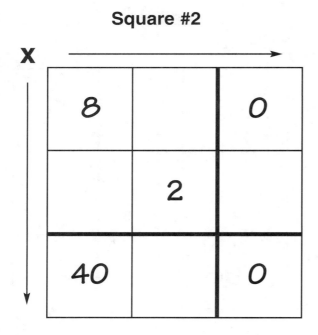

X →		
8		0
	2	
40		0

Square #3

X →		
15		60
	5	
45		900

Answer Key

Page 4
1. 276
2. 61
3. 977
4. 810
5. 954

Page 5
1. Shep eats hot dogs and drinks milk.
2. Jay eats hamburgers and drinks shakes.
3. Tina eats tacos and drinks water.
4. Marie eats pizza and drinks soda.

Page 6
Across
1. seventeen
6. eleven
8. thirteen
9. eighteen
10. twenty

Down
1. sixteen
2. twelve
3. fifteen
4. fourteen
5. ten
7. nineteen

Page 7
1. 7
2. 12
3. 12
4. 13
5. 3
6. 2
7. 60
8. 24
9. 2 or 3
10. 144
11. 5 or 9
12. 5
13. 10
14. 13
15. 50
16. 10
17. 365
18. 366
19. 5
20. 2
21. $12 \div 12 = 1$
22. $60 \div 3 = 20$
23. $366 - 365 = 1$
24. $10 \times 2 = 20$
25. $13 \times 7 = 91$
26. $10 \div 5 = 2$
27. $144 + 2 =$ (or 3) = 146 (or 147)
28. $24 - 5 = 19$

Page 8
1. $12 + 23 + 11 + 14 + 22 + 24 = 106$
2. $16 + 1 + 11 + 14 + 22 + 24 = 88$
3. $17 + 23 + 19 + 12 + 14 + 22 + 24 = 131$
4. $18 + 19 + 14 + 11 + 19 + 12 + 14 + 22 + 24 = 153$
5. $17 + 25 + 23 + 2 + 12 + 14 + 22 + 24 = 139$
6. $26 + 2 + 15 + 14 + 22 + 24 = 103$
7. $12 + 22 + 17 + 23 + 2 + 14 + 22 + 24 = 136$
8. $106 \times 4 - 139 = 285$
9. $136 - 131 \times 20 = 100$
10. $153 - 103 \div 10 = 5$
11. $88 \div 4 \times 106 = 2,332$
12. $(136 - 103) + (153 - 88) = 33 + 65 = 98$

Page 9
Color blue: 71, 11, 31, 53, 29, 47, 73, 7, 5, 13, 3, 1, 43, 23, 59, 17, 19, 61, 79, 67, 41, 37 (The picture will show a happy face.)

Page 10
1. 28, 33, 38, 43, 48, 53
   Rule: Add 5
2. 17, 15, 13, 11, 9, 7
   Rule: Subtract 2
3. 51, 47, 43, 39, 35, 31
   Rule: Subtract 4
4. 75, 83, 91, 99, 107, 115 Rule: Add 8
5. 85, 97, 109, 121, 133, 145 Rule: Add 12
6. 99, 109, 119, 129, 139, 149 Rule: Add 10
7. 43, 50, 57, 64, 71, 78
   Rule: Add 7

Page 11
1. Multiply by 2 or double each number
2. Multiply by 5
3. Divide by 3
4. Divide by 2
5. Multiply by 4
6. Multiply by 10

Page 12
1. 4
2. $0.10
3. Yes
4. An extra album page
5. $7.75

Page 13
1. $19.35
2. $18.52
3. $15.73
4. $15.76
5. $13.69
6. $14.94

Page 14
1. Ryan
2. Sarah
3. Sybil
4. Janice
5. Robin
6. Christopher
7. Cheryl
8. Bonnie

Page 15
A1. $0.54
A2. 4 pennies, 1 half-dollar
B1. $0.66
B2. 1 penny, 4 nickels, 2 dimes, 1 quarter
C1. $1.18
C2. 3 pennies, 1 nickel, 1 dime, 2 quarters, 1 half-dollar
D1. $2.43
D2. 3 pennies, 1 nickel, 1 dime, 1 quarter, 4 half-dollars

Page 16
A1. $0.80
A2. $0.20
B1. $0.85
B2. $0.15
C1. $1.20
C2. $0.30
D1. $4.75
D2. $0.25
E1. $1.70
E2. $0.30
F1. $0.50
F2. $0.50

Page 17
Example: 7 nickels or $.35
1. 1 nickel or $0.05
2. 2 nickels or $0.10
3. 4 nickels or $0.20

Page 18
4. 11 nickels or $0.55
5. 11 nickels or $0.55
6. 6 nickels or $0.30
7. 8 nickels or $0.40
8. 5 nickels or $0.25
9. 8 nickels or $0.40

Page 19
1. $6 \times \$0.20 = \$1.20$ or $15 \times \$0.05 = \$0.75$
   Circle 6 quarters.
   The difference is $0.45.
2. $8 \times \$0.20 = \$1.60$ or $2 \times \$0.85 = \$1.70$
   Circle two $1.00 bills.
   The difference is $0.10.
3. $1 \times \$4.75 = \$4.75$ or $5 \times \$0.85 = \$4.25$
   Circle $5.00 bill.
   The difference is $0.50.
4. $1 \times \$9.80 = \$9.80$ or $10 \times \$0.85 = \$8.50$
   Circle $10.00 bill.
   The difference is $1.30.
5. $1 \times \$19.50 = \$19.50$ or $2 \times \$9.80 = \$19.60$
   Circle two $10.00 bills.
   The difference is $0.10.

Page 20
Circles of Challenge #1
A = 100
B = 50
C = 75
D = 25
E = 125

Circles of Challenge #2
A = 300
B = 100
C = 200
D = 400
E = 500

Page 21
Circles of Challenge #3
A = 20
B = 19
C = 18
D = 17
E = 16

Circles of Challenge #4
A = 50
B = 30
C = 20
D = 40
E = 10

Page 22
Circles of Challenge #5
A = 15
B = 20
C = 0
D = 10
E = 5

Circles of Challenge #6
A = 50
B = 250
C = 100
D = 200
E = 150

Page 23
Circles of Challenge #7
A = 3	D = 2
B = 4	E = 5
C = 1	

Circles of Challenge #8
A = 2	D = 6
B = 10	E = 8
C = 4	

Page 24
Circles of Challenge #9
A = 5	D = 20
B = 15	E = 10
C = 25	

Circles of Challenge #10
A = 50	D = 20
B = 30	E = 40
C = 10	

Page 25
Circles of Challenge #11
A = 32	D = 4
B = 8	E = 2
C = 16	

Circles of Challenge #12
A = 36	D = 12
B = 6	E = 3
C = 24	

Page 26
1. 60	5. 55	8. 53
2. 52	6. 54	9. 57
3. 59	7. 51	10. 58
4. 56		

Page 27
1. 100	5. 98	8. 92
2. 93	6. 99	9. 97
3. 96	7. 91	10. 94
4. 95		

Page 28
1. x, −, +, ÷
2. ÷, −, x, +
3. x, ÷, −, +
4. −, x, +, ÷
5. −, ÷, +, x
6. x, +, ÷, −
7. −, ÷, x, +
8. +, −, ÷, x

Page 29
1. +, x, ÷ , −
2. −, ÷, +, x
3. ÷, −, +, x
4. −, ÷, x, +
5. x, −, ÷, +
6. ÷, +, x, −
7. +, −, ÷, x
8. −, ÷, x, +

Page 30
The mystery number is 29.

Page 31
The mystery number is 56.

Page 32
The mystery number is 541.

Page 33
The mystery number is 1,052.

Page 34
The mystery number is 10,289.

Page 35
6:	VI
2:	II
1:	I
12:	XII
15:	XV
86:	LXXXVI
21:	XXI
60:	LX
73:	LXXIII
815:	DCCCXV
281:	CCLXXXI
356:	CCCLVI
686:	DCLXXXVI
783:	DCCLXXXIII
127:	CXXVII
770:	DCCLXX
530:	DXXX
762:	DCCLXII
2,163:	MMCLXIII
3,573:	MMMDLXXIII
3,107:	MMMCVII
1,078:	MLXXVIII
2,510:	MMDX
3,898:	MMMDCCCXCVIII
4,103:	MMMMCIII
1,200:	MCC

Page 36
1. 4	10. 509
2. 14	11. 154
3. 24	12. 109
4. 48	13. 104
5. 95	14. 900
6. 40	15. 400
7. 90	16. 1,029
8. 64	17. 804
9. 69	18. 554
A. XXIV	
B. XC	
C. XXXIX	
D. XLI	

Page 37
1. To count by 2s
2. To count by 5s
3. To count by 3s
4. To count by 10s
5. To count by 8s
6. To count by 50s
7. To multiply by 2 or double each number

Page 38
1. 4,517	7. 8,147
2. 13,066	8. 6,734
3. 11,974	9. 7,692
4. 18,557	10. 2,735
5. 4,751	11. 11,870
6. 13,095	

Movie: The Great Train Robbery

Page 39
1. 9,312	6. 10,904
2. 12,684	7. 16,866
3. 4,902	8. 10,192
4. 2,956	9. 13,324
5. 17,426	10. 12,129

Cartoon: Steamboat Willie

Page 40
1. 7 + 3 + 7 + 3 = 20 units; 3 x 7 = 21 sq. units
2. 9 + 3 + 9 + 3 = 24 units; 9 x 3 = 27 sq. units
3. 3 + 3 + 3 + 3 = 12 units; 3 x 3 = 9 sq. units
4. 8 + 2 + 8 + 2 = 20 units; 8 x 2 = 16 sq. units
5. 9 + 2 + 9 + 2 = 22 units; 9 x 2 = 18 sq. units

Page 41
1. B and E	3. A
2. C	4. D

Page 42
1. 1/2 gallon
2. 5 gallons
3. 1 gallon
4. 5 gallons

Page 43
Square #1:
Top Row: 6
Middle Row: 10, 5
Bottom Row: 3

Square #2
Top Row: 20
Middle Row: 25, 5
Bottom Row: 4

Square #3
Top Row: 8
Middle Row: 4, 2
Bottom Row: 4

Page 44
Square #1
Top Row: 16
Middle Row: 8, 2
Bottom Row: 4

Square #2
Top Row: 40
Middle Row: 60, 3
Bottom Row: 2

Square #3
Top Row: 50
Middle Row: 40, 4
Bottom Row: 5

Page 45
Square #1
Top Row: 7
Middle Row: 6, 30
Bottom Row: 35

Square #2
Top Row: 2
Middle Row: 4, 24
Bottom Row: 12

Square #3
Top Row: 1
Middle Row: 11, 33
Bottom Row: 3

Page 46
Square #1
Top Row: 3
Middle Row: 4, 4
Bottom Row: 3

Square #2
Top Row: 0
Middle Row: 5, 10
Bottom Row: 0

Square #3
Top Row: 4
Middle Row: 3, 15
Bottom Row: 20